AF265877

Published by too-woo.com

2nd Edition 2015

ISBN: 978-0-9934145-0-3

EXPLORING WITH TOO WOO

The magical world of Butterflies

DEDICATION

This book is for my wonderful wife Aselle for all her support.

&

for Tim Johnson (www.thelanguagebear.com), who inspired
me to complete something I started 25 years ago.

ACKNOWLEDGEMENTS

Lynn Smith-Davies' editing skills (and patience) turned my weird structure and at times, bizarre punctuation into a coherent story, I can't thank her enough.

I have consulted numerous both printed and web sources in writing this book, cross checking information, sometimes, a dozen times. Although this small book is not meant to be scientific, I have tried to make it accurate – any errors are entirely mine. There is a list of useful books and web sites on page 20.

Dictionaries consulted are: Oxford English, Cambridge Advanced learners, Miriam Webster, Dictionary.com, Origins Etymological Dictionary of Modern English, The Online Etymology Dictionary and the American Heritage Dictionary.

EXPLORING WITH TOO WOO

The magical world of Butterflies

Written and Illustrated by

Evelyn Wood

Evelyn Wood

TOO WOO and the magical world of Butterflies

I'm Too Woo and this is the story of Butterflies. They are amazing creatures who start life as tiny eggs, hatch as caterpillars that eat and eat and eat until they turn into chrysalides and then become butterflies.

Learn some neat facts and new words that are explained on page 12.

There is a story about a greedy spider too.

I'll be your guide as we explore.

You can visit me at www.too-woo.com/

1

There are between 15 and 20,000 types of butterflies in the world but only 340 breeds of dogs and about 70 breeds of cats - that's amazing!

The butterfly chooses a strong happy plant, and lays about 200 eggs under a leaf to hide them.

She does this to protect them but only about 10 survive! The others die from wind or rain or are eaten.

The egg is the size of a pinhead• (2 mm); the baby caterpillar hatches after a week and is this big ▬(3 mm).

They are fussy about food and most types will only eat one kind of plant.

Caterpillars eat their eggshell first and then just eat leaves and eat and eat until in 2 to 3 weeks, they grow to this size (50 mm).

"Stop eating me – you're so greedy! Since you popped out of your egg you haven't stopped eating," complains the flower.

"I'm not greedy, I'm hungry" says the caterpillar.

The flower is very cross "You'd make a tasty snack for birds, lizards, spiders, wasps, flies, beetles and many other creatures who are hungry too".

"Oh no!" cries the caterpillar.

She's lucky her mother chose an area where ants protect her in exchange for the sweet liquid on her skin.

Brave ants fight a wasp whilst the caterpillar hides.

Some caterpillars disguise themselves with scary marks or even eat things that make them poisonous or smell disgusting to fool hungry enemies.

We've seen how quickly caterpillars grow,
what if you did the same?

You would be 8 meters tall = 26 feet.
(That's like an Indian elephant standing on a bus.)

And you'd weigh 1.5 tons like the Lady Hippo.

Imagine that!

Butterflies are insects. Insects have six legs but caterpillars have 16. On their thorax, they have six real legs; the eight on their abdomen and two at the end are called "prolegs" they are used to walk on plants. When the caterpillar becomes a chrysalis, it loses the prolegs.

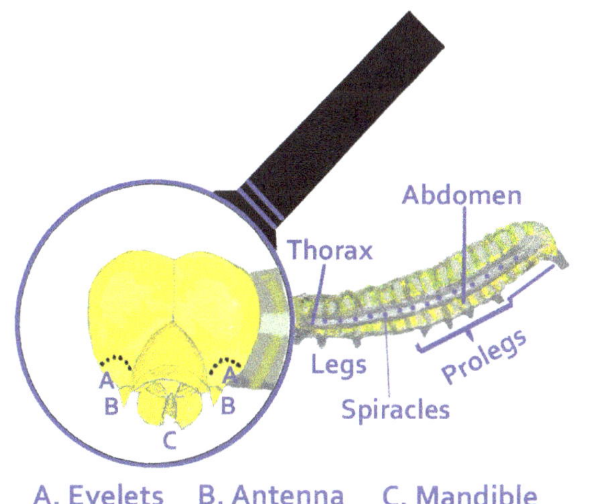

A. Eyelets   B. Antenna   C. Mandible

Together with its 16 legs, it has 12 eyelets but you need a magnifying glass to see them.

Even with 12 eyes, it does not see very well and uses hairs called setae, all over its body as sensors.

The mandibles are strong jaws for tearing up leaves before they go to the mouth. (You have teeth for this).

Have you noticed the caterpillar does not have a nose? It uses its antenna to smell and special pores on the chest and stomach, called spiracles, to breathe.

As a caterpillar grows, it has to take off its skin.   That's because its exoskeleton can't grow. So, instead of bursting with a POP, they molt four or five times by wriggling out of their skin and growing a new one. With each molt stage, or Instar, they get bigger.

After 2 to 3 weeks, when the caterpillar has grown big enough, it's ready to start turning into a butterfly.

Metamorphosis starts with the last molting and the caterpillar pupating.

KNOWLEDGE BOX

Caterpillars don't have a skeleton. Instead, they have an "exoskeleton" a Greek word meaning "outer skeleton".

Butterfly and moth caterpillars can make silk. They are relatives but moths are awake at night and, like you, butterflies are awake in the day.

The silk we wear comes from the silkworm. It's not a worm but the caterpillar of Bombyx mori and it only eats mulberry leaves.

When Butterfly caterpillars pupate, they hang from a thread of silk and make a chrysalis with their final exoskeleton.

Moth caterpillars spin a cocoon of silk and change into a moth inside that. The silk we wear is made from silkworm cocoons.

The caterpillar makes silk and ties itself to a leaf or twig.

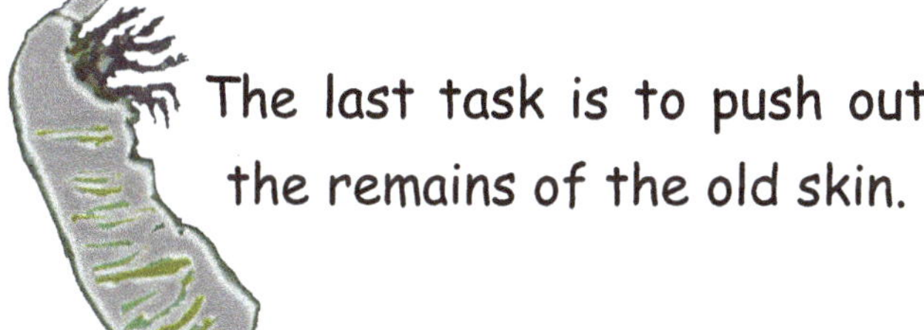

After one to two days hanging upside down, the caterpillar starts wriggling like crazy.

Then the caterpillar's skin splits open for the last time.

The caterpillar makes its chrysalis by shedding its old skin - here it's half way through.

The last task is to push out the remains of the old skin.

The new skin hardens and becomes the chrysalis.

When the chrysalis is complete, the magic starts! The pupa melts itself with a special chemical and becomes a soup inside the chrysalis. Floating in it are the imaginal discs, these are tiny patterns for each part of the butterfly and the pupa uses them, and the soup, to change into a butterfly.

It generally takes one to two weeks to change, although some types take months.

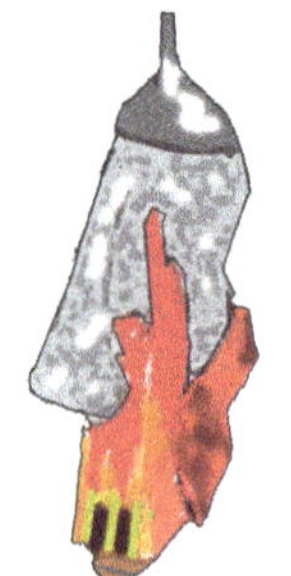

When the magical changes of metamorphosis have finished, it's time for the butterfly to break out of its chrysalis. It starts by releasing a chemical that softens the chrysalis. When the case is soft, the butterfly can start pushing out.

It hangs from the chrysalis and pumps liquid into the veins of its wings to stretch them. The wings are made from a transparent material called chitin, which is similar to keratin that your hair and nails are made from.

While they wait for their wings to dry, they clean their feet and faces and join their proboscis (which is in two halves) using hooks like Velcro to make a drinking tube.

Now our butterflies can go on a test flight; top speed 12 miles (19 km) an hour.

Butterfly food is nectar and water (especially if it has minerals), which they drink through their proboscis, it's like a drinking straw that they carry coiled up like a spring.

They don't have a mouth and only drink, so they can pee but not poop!

Butterflies breathe through spiracles like caterpillars and have an exoskeleton but in other ways they are very different from them and not just because they have wings.

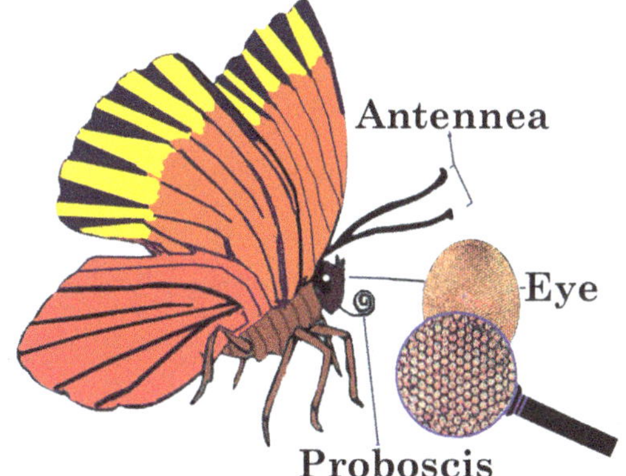

Butterflies have special eyes with between 12,000 and 17,000 microscopic lenses each, as shown in the magnifying glass. They can see flower patterns that are invisible to humans, which help them find nectar that they taste with their feet!

Butterflies range in size from 1/8 inch to 12 inches (3 mm to 30 cm) and their two antennae are used like radar to keep their balance. They cannot close their eyes and can't sleep, although they do rest. They have four wings, two forewings, which look a bit like triangles close to the head, and two fan-shaped hindwings. Their wings have tiny scales, giving them their color and patterns.

The patterns are used to identify and attract a mate, and as camouflage. Butterflies are brilliant at hiding themselves and creating patterns like scary eyes to frighten away predators.

Butterflies are cold blooded creatures. That means if it gets too cold, they can't move and need to roost in a warm place before their legs and wings work again.

Sometimes, on a warm winter's day they are fooled and wake too early, which is bad if it gets cold again.

Different species have their own ways of surviving winter. Some lay eggs that hatch in spring in a protected place. Others hibernate as caterpillars or pupa in a safe place. Some hibernate as butterflies, usually in the bark of trees or in a building.

The last strategy is migration to a warm climate. More than 200 butterfly species migrate over long distances. The best known is the Monarch butterfly, which, in groups of multiple generations, may travel as much as 2,500 miles (4,023 KM).

Migration is amazing but what about space butterflies?

In an exciting event in their short lives, Monarch & Painted Lady butterflies became the first in space when caterpillars pupated and then emerged from their chrysalides on the international space station in 2009.

Space station commander Jeff Williams said the astronauts were happy too, having something real from earth flying around their space ship.

A butterfly lives between a week and a year, depending on the species and spends its life drinking, pollinating plants, finding a mate and laying eggs, perhaps on the same flower where it started life.

As you see, the flower has recovered from being eaten.

Hundreds of years ago scientists got fed up with different names for the same thing. It confused them. In 1735, Carl von Linné, a Swedish scientist, created a naming system called "Binomial nomenclature" it is based mainly on Latin, a language educated people everywhere understood.

The word Lepidoptera is Greek and means scale winged.

All butterflies and moths belong to the Lepidoptera family.

The Turkish for Monarch Butterfly is "Kral kelebeği" but all scientists know that the Latin "Danaus plexippus" is a Monarch butterfly.

This clever idea means scientists can understand each other because they have common languages, Greek and Latin. The words describe the look or action of the part described. In the table below are other words you'll find in the story. The words are basic and tell us about a part of the insect. Sometimes, it's a word picture like antenna because on insects it looks like the horizontal yard on a ship's mast from which the sails are set. Chrysalis, plural chrysalides, is the hardened case of the pupa.

Below are Latin words we've used.

Abdomen = Belly	Imaginal discs = Image	Pupate and Pupa = Doll
Antenna = Sail Yard (wow!)	Instar = Form or likeness	Setae = Bristle
Bombyx mori = Silkworm Moth	Mandible = Jaw Chew	Spiracles = Air Hole
Cocoon = Protective silk case	Predator = Plunderer	Thorax = Breast Plate
Hibernate = Spend the Winter	Proboscis = Feeding tube	Migrate = Change abode

What's in Too Woo's bag?

These items help you explore, keep you safe and make sure you don't get hungry or thirsty. You can add other items too!

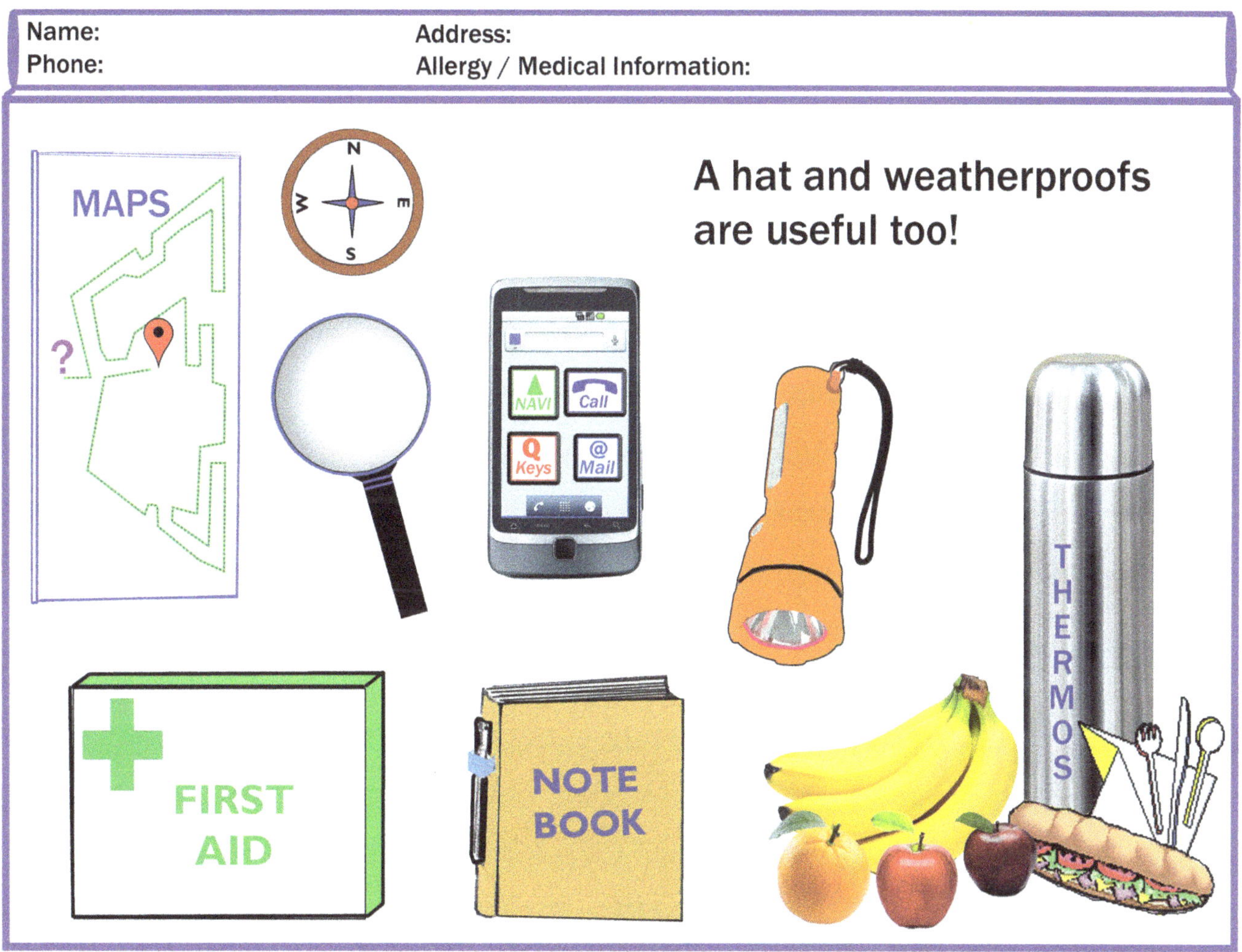

A butterfly told me this story about a greedy spider.

Flying along one day, the butterfly was caught in a web.

The butterfly tried to flap her wings, first one, then the other; both were stuck.

"Gotcha" yelled the Spider.

"Who are you?" asked the Butterfly.

"I'm the Spider who's caught you in his web and I'm going to eat you!"

The Butterfly tried to free herself but a passing fly shouted, "Don't struggle, it will make it worse". 

The Spider walked towards her, snapping his teeth.

" You're fat" she remarked.

The spider stopped and stared. "How rude you are, one should never comment on someone's size."

"You want to eat me, that's ruder than saying you're fat. You're not just fat you're sweating too".

The Spider was furious. "How dare you," he shouted "how dare you say such horrid things!".

The Butterfly kept calm and soothingly remarked, "I only said them to be helpful. It's well known that sweaty people don't really enjoy their food". She paused and smiled bravely at him. "And if I'm to be eaten I'd like to be enjoyed, that's fair isn't it?"

The spider sat down and scratched his head.

"Well   it's true that I don't really enjoy my food and I am hot, but I'm hungry too, so what can I do?"

"Well" said the Butterfly, "I could fan you and make you cool."

"Fan me?" questioned the Spider.

"Yes, just release one of my wings and I'll fan you".

"If I do that you'll run away".

"How could I? One wing will still be trapped ".

The spider thought a long thought. "Well, if you promise not to run away".

"I promise," she said.

The spider cut the web from around one of her wings so that she could flap it.

"Oh that is good, really excellent! But I could do with it being a little stronger".

"If you release the other wing it will be twice as good" said the butterfly.

"Twice as good", mused the Spider "twice as good, twice as good... and you prom...." "Yes, I promise not to run away," the butterfly interrupted.

The spider cut the other wing free and she beat her wings very fast.

"Oh, that's wonderful, so cooling, so refreshing, so appetising." He looked greedily at her just as she lifted off from the web.

"Come back" he shouted "you promised".

"I promised not to run away and I'm not, I'm flying away".

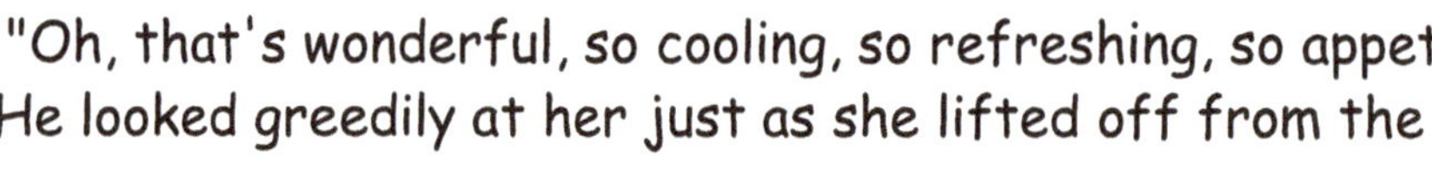

She settled safely on a nearby flower and thirstily drank from its nectar.

The Spider was beside himself with rage "You cheat!" he yelled. "You cheat! I'll never trust another butterfly, never!"

He raged, stamped and fumed, making such a noise that it warned everyone to steer clear of his web.

That night the Butterfly slept in a foxglove, happy and content.

The Spider went to bed hungry!

Quiz!

Can you answer these questions?

1. How many types of butterfly are there?
2. What creatures might eat the caterpillar?
3. Do you know some ways it protects itself?
4. If you grew like a caterpillar how tall would you be?
5. What would you weigh the same as?
6. How many legs does a caterpillar have?
7. How does a caterpillar smell its food?
8. What does the caterpillar shed when it grows?
9. How does the caterpillar change into a butterfly?
10. How fast can a butterfly fly?
11. Can the butterfly poop?
12. How do butterflies survive the winter?
13. How do butterflies taste their food?
14. What did Carl von Linné create?

Answers on page 21.

Design your own Caterpillar and Butterfly

What would your butterfly look like? Here are some shapes for you to color.

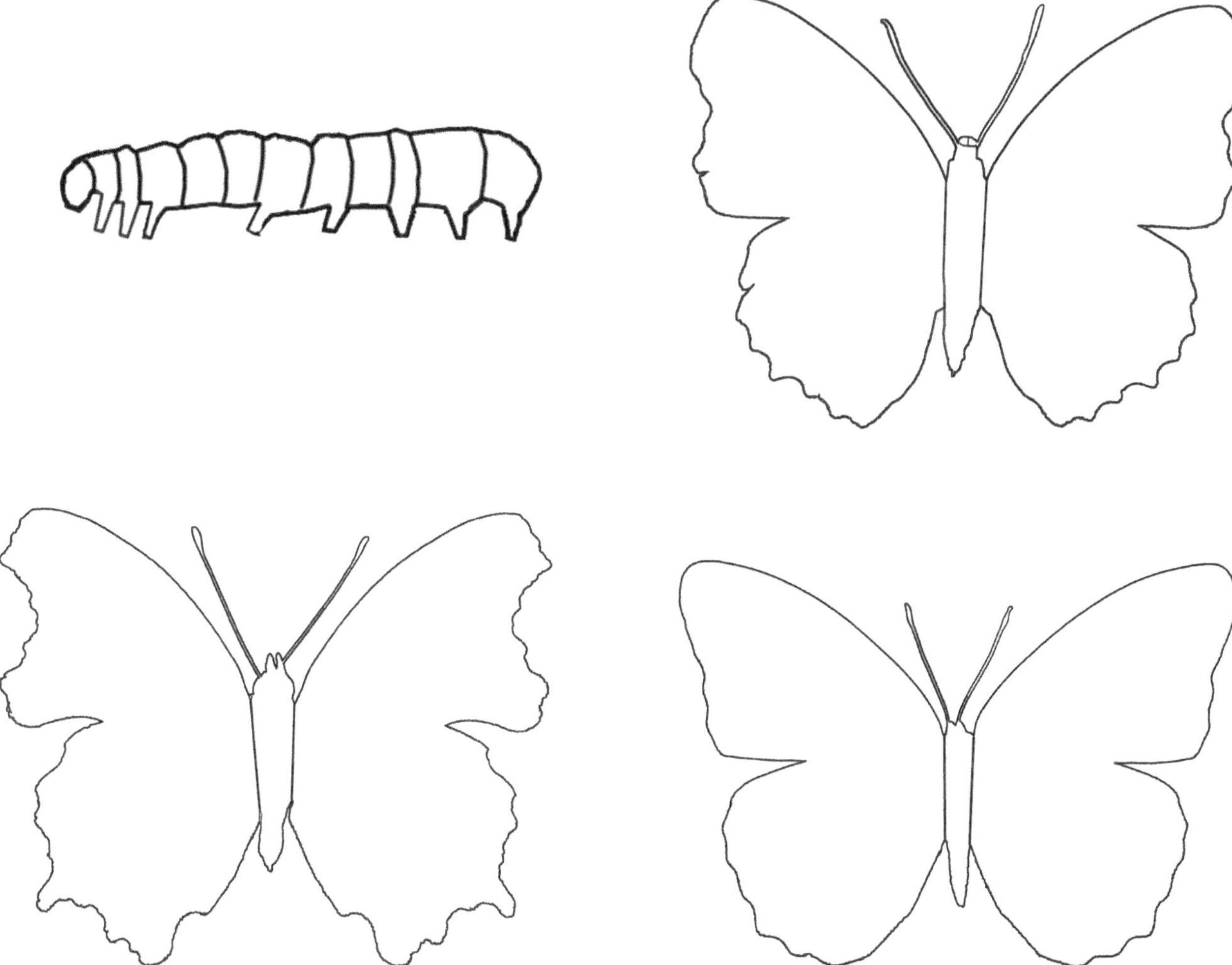

These are a few resources to help you explore more.

Books:

1. The Illustrated World Encyclopaedia of Butterflies & Moths: by Sally Morgan. Hardcover, 256 pages Lorenz Books ISBN 0754818845 (ISBN 13: 9780754818847)

2. Smithsonian Handbooks: Butterflies & Moths: DK. Paperback: 304 pages. ISBN-10: 078948983X ISBN-13: 978-0789489838

3. Collins Butterfly Guide: The Most Complete Guide to the Butterflies of Britain and Europe by Tom Tolman 384 pages: ISBN-10 0007279779 ISBN-13 9780007279777

4. The Complete Book of North American Butterflies by Dr Paul A Opler. Advantage Publishers Group: Paperback: 192 pages ISBN-10: 1607102765 ISBN-13: 978-1607102762

Web Sites:

A. http://www.lepsoc.org/lepidoptera_websites_1.php   The Lepidopterists' Society in the USA is an excellent resource for those interested in Butterflies and has an educational section. It has an exhaustive list of web sites about Butterflies and Moths.

B. http://www.discoverlife.org/ is a wonderful resource on the natural world.

C. http://www.lepidoptera.eu/ is a resource for European butterflies listed by Country.

D. http://www.learnaboutbutterflies.com/index.htm Is a website created and maintained by Adrian Hoskins a Butterfly expert and enthusiast. It has many photos and aids to identify species.

QUIZ ANSWERS

1. Between 15 and 20,000.
2. Birds, lizards, spiders, wasps, flies, beetles and more.
3. Ants protection, disguise and smelling bad.
4. 8 meters = 26 feet.
5. A lady Hippo.
6. 16.
7. With its antenna.
8. Its skin.
9. Metamorphosis. It changes inside its Chrysalis.
10. 12 miles (19 KM) an hour.
11. No.
12. Hibernation or migration.
13. With their feet.
14. A system of scientific naming.

ABOUT THE AUTHOR

As a boy, I spent hours watching the Puss Moth caterpillars that lived on the Willow tree in our garden. They are handsome creatures and, I was told, could spray acid from their two tails if attacked. This early fascination stayed with me during a career in agriculture and business. I've been fortunate to have lived and worked in a number of countries in Europe, Africa and Asia each with wonderful fauna and flora to discover. I hope this small book will spark a similar interest in children keen to explore the natural world.

I now live in London and fill my days writing, painting and cooking. I am still as curious as when I was young and believe no one should go to bed until they have learned one new skill or fact during that day.

My Notes

Use this space to record where you were and the date you saw the butterfly or its caterpillar and its name.

If you have a separate Note Book, like Too Woo, you can arrange it as you'd like. Maybe with a drawing too?

DATE	WHERE	NAME